Unending
P·R·A·I·S·E

*A fabric of contemporary favorites
arranged for organ by Tim Doran*

Lillenas PUBLISHING COMPANY

KANSAS CITY, MO 64141

CONTENTS

In Sequence

CONTENTS

Alphabetical

In Moments Like These

Swell: Oboe 8', trem.
Great: Str. celeste 8'
Pedal: Bourdon 16', 8'

DAVID GRAHAM
Arr. by Tim Doran

6

Song ending

Opt. transition ending

rit.

Gt.

Calvary's Love

Swell: Oboe 8'
Great: Str. celeste 8'
Pedal: Bourdon 16', 8'

GREG NELSON and PHILL McHUGH
Arr. by Tim Doran

There Is a Redeemer

Swell: Diapason 8'
Great: Tpt. 8', trem.
Pedal: Bourdon 16', 8'

MELODY GREEN
Arr. by Tim Doran

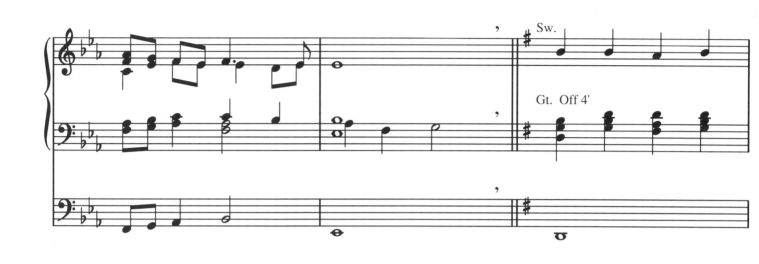

Lord of All

Swell: Diap. 8', Fl. 8'
Great: Str. celeste 8', 4'
Pedal: Bourdon 16', 8'

PHILL McHUGH
Arr. by Tim Doran

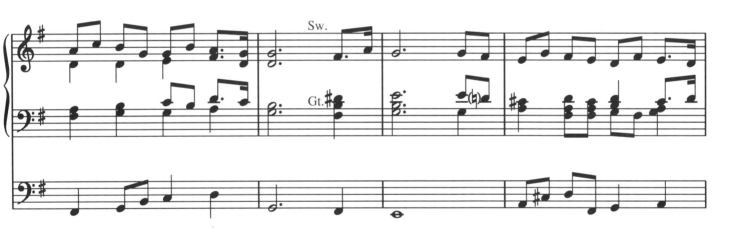

14

Gt. Full, Add Prin. 8'

Sw.

Gt. Str. celeste only

Song ending

Opt. transition ending

rit.

Lord of My Heart

Great: Fl. 8', 4', trem.
Pedal: Bourdon 16', 8'

TWILA PARIS
Arr. by Tim Doran

Only Jesus

Great: Str. celeste 8'
Pedal: Bourdon 16', 8'

GREG NELSON and PHILL McHUGH
Arr. by Tim Doran

Thou Art Worthy

Swell: Clarinet 8'
Great: Str. celeste 8'
Pedal: Bourdon 16', 8'

PAULINE M. MILLS
Arr. by Tim Doran

As the Deer

Swell: Ged. 8', 2'
Great: Str. celeste 8', 4'
Pedal: Bourdon 16', 8'

MARTIN NYSTROM
Arr. by Tim Doran

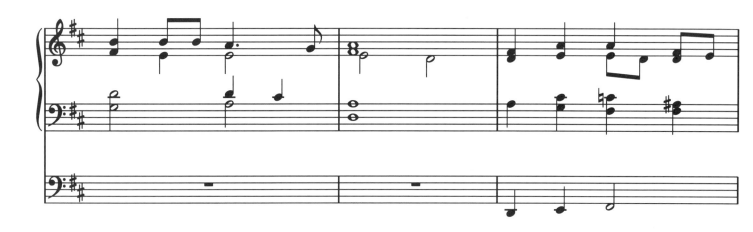

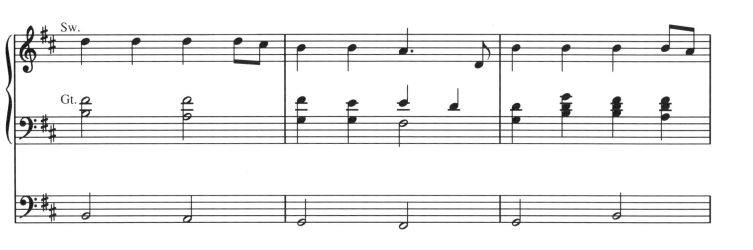

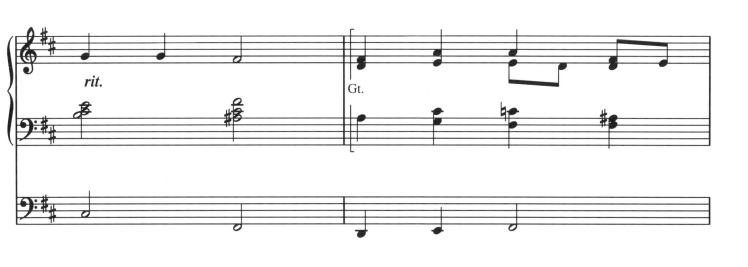

Lamb of Glory

Swell: Oboe 8', trem.
Great: Str. celeste 8'
Pedal: Bourdon 16', 8'

GREG NELSON and PHILL McHUGH
Arr. by Tim Doran

a tempo

Gt. Add Prin. 8'

Off Prin. 8'

molto rit.

Give Thanks

Swell: Ged. 8', Naz. 2 2/3'
Great: Str. celeste 8'
Pedal: Bourdon 16', 8'

HENRY SMITH
Arr. by Tim Doran

We Bring the Sacrifice of Praise

Swell: Tpt. 8', 4'
Great: Prin. 8'
Pedal: Bourdon 16', 8'

KIRK DEARMAN
Arr. by Tim Doran

Sw. Tpt. 8', trem.

Gt. Str. celeste 8' only

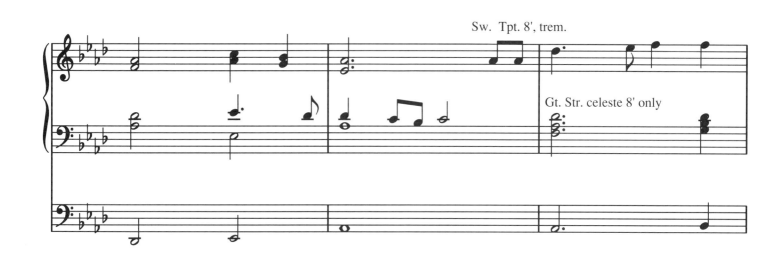

rit.

Bless God

Great: Str. celeste 8', 4'
Pedal: Bourdon 16', 8'

CARMAN LICCIARDELLO
Arr. by Tim Doran

How Excellent Is Thy Name

Swell: Tpt. 8', 4'
Great: Prin. 8', 4', 2'
Pedal: Bourdon 16', 4'

MELODY and DICK TUNNEY, PAUL C. SMITH
Arr. by Tim Doran

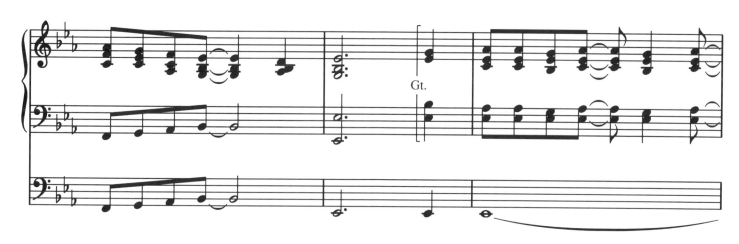

Sw. Tpt. 8', 4'. Off trem.

Gt. Off 2'

rit.

Jesus, Name Above All Names

Great: Str. celeste 8'
Pedal: Bourdon 16', 8'

NAIDA HEARN
Arr. by Tim Doran

His Name Is Life

Swell: Clar. 8', trem.
Great: Str. celeste 8', 4'
Pedal: Bourdon 16', 8'

WILLIAM J. GAITHER and CARMAN LICCIARDELLO
Arr. by Tim Doran

Holy Ground

Great: Full, with celestes
Pedal: Bourdon 16', 8'

GERON DAVIS
Arr. by Tim Doran

We Worship and Adore You

Swell: Oboe 8', trem.
Great: Str. celeste 8', Diap. celeste 8'
Pedal: Bourdon 16', 8'

ANONYMOUS
Arr. by Tim Doran

There Is a Savior

Swell: Clar. 8', trem.
Great: Str. celeste 8'
Pedal: Bourdon 16', 8'

BOB FARRELL, SANDI PATTI
HELVERING, and GREG NELSON
Arr. by Tim Doran

Great Is the Lord

Swell: Reed chorus, full
Great: Full 8', 4', 2'
Pedal: Bourdon 16', 8', full

MICHAEL W. and DEBORAH D. SMITH
Arr. by Tim Doran

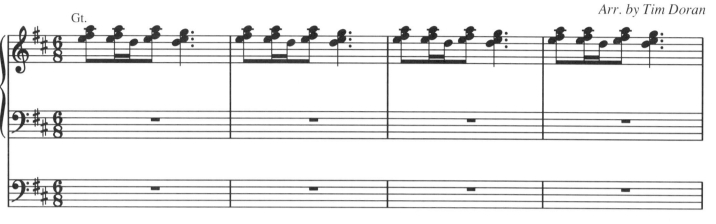

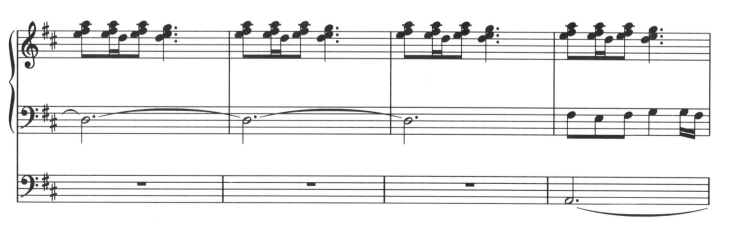

Praise You, I Will Praise You

Swell: Tpt. 8' (or full reeds)
Great: Prin. 8', 4'
Pedal: Diap. 8', 4'

MICHAEL W. SMITH
Arr. by Tim Doran

All Hail King Jesus

Swell: Flute 8'
Great: Full, with celeste and mixtures
Pedal: Bourdon 16'

DAVE MOODY
Arr. by Tim Doran

Gt. Add reeds (off celeste)

Add cresc. pedal